LAURIE and HER

VINEYARD LADIES

by Lee DeVitt

How the Minis Found Homes on Martha's Vineyard

I DEDICATE THIS BOOK TO LAURIE AND ALL OTHERS
INVOLVED WITH HELPING ANIMALS.

I give grateful thanks to the following: Laurie, for all help as well as her photos,
both old and recent; Julia Humphreys, for her interest in and photos of the minis;
Penny Uhlendorf, for her recent photos of Laurie's girls and her work on the
Foundation; for Patty DeVitt Blakesley for her original idea and her photographs;
Janet Holladay, for her expert prepress aid, and all the Tisbury Printer
staff for their interest and work on the book.

Copyright © 2005 TURTLE TOO Press
ISBN 0-9769586-0-0

20 School House Village Vineyard Haven, MA 02568

Vineyard Miniature Horse Rescue, Inc. P.O. Box 199 · Vineyard Haven · MA 02568

Printed in Canada

This book is based on the true tale of one young lady. I hope her story will inspire others to follow their dreams – to improve their own immediate world and to help others.

Laurie happened to choose to help animals. Half of any profit from the sale of this book will go to the Foundation set up for her selfless work with her ladies that you can read about on the following pages.

Enter LAURIE'S WORLD...

When Laurie was a little girl she lived in a friendly neighborhood on Tashmoo Avenue in Tisbury on the island of Martha's Vineyard, Massachusetts. She always wanted a dog or a horse of her own. She did not have either, but everyday that she could, she took Dundee for a walk. He was a collie who belonged to her neighbors, and she treated him like he was her own.

She did have parakeets, but no other animals considered and sold as normal pets. So she made cages and tried to make natural homes or aquariums to keep other living things she found. These included frogs, salamanders, turtles, bugs of all kinds and even worms.

She recalls that she saved, or tried to save, hundreds of baby birds. A tree trimmer for the town was a friend of hers, and when he had to take a branch down that held a nest of baby birds, he made certain that Laurie received them. Then she got worms from Gus Ben David to feed them. Gus Ben David, Director of Massachusetts Audubon Felix Neck Sanctuary, was her hero. Laurie was a day camper there in the summertime, and her heart just opened up to all animals. Her love for them grew as she did.

When Laurie was in 8th grade she was given riding lessons at Featherstone Farm in Oak Bluffs.

Her family could only afford one lesson a month, which was $4.00 for an hour. Laurie loved horses even then and sometimes would rake her Mother's lawn for extra lessons. Her favorite horse to ride was Major, a large strawberry roan gelding. A gelding is a male horse that has been neutered, and, thus, is usually considered more gentle for young riders. Strawberry refers to the light reddish brown of Major's base coat. Roan horses have gray or white hairs mixed in or as spots in their base coat.

Laurie was able to buy her own horse when she was 19. Harvey was an old, palomino gelding. In the summer he was the color of a new copper penny and his mane and tail were blonde, but in the winter he was blonde all over. Laurie kept him near Authier's Way

which at that time was a field with a barn. They were a familiar sight when she rode him all over West Chop. Later she returned him to the man in Connecticut from whom she had bought him as that man also ran a retirement farm for horses. Perhaps that always stayed in her mind –– that someone who loved horses took care of those that owners no longer could care for.

Cinnamini

Several years ago, by chance, Laurie read about a dealer in Maine in a want ad magazine. He bought and sold cattle and had purchased a lot from South Dakota. It included a lone miniature horse. She thought that was strange and did not like the idea of the little horse being in the lot of cattle to be auctioned off, possibly for the meat market.

So when she found out the dealer would sell it separately, she made arrangements to buy it and have it shipped from Maine to Martha's Vineyard. Then she had to find a pasture, with a shed, that she could rent. And so Cinnamini from South Dakota - so named because of her sorrel color and her friendliness - became the first of Laurie's ladies. She is the only one with a nickname and that varies from Cinnamini to Cinnaminiwhinney.

To this day Cinnamini remains one of the horses most interested in people and in joining whatever is going on. Laurie finds that each of the ladies have their own personality. Depending how they have been treated in the past, they may be aggressive to the others or shy. Some are skittish and timid or hard to handle when Laurie tries to put on a halter because of previous abuse they have received. Just as people vary in personality and behavior, so do the little horses.

Cinnamini

Apple Dumplin'

Laurie's second lady is a seal brown miniature named Apple Dumplin'. She is the oldest of all the group, being 26 years of age. Several things helped Laurie to decide on rescuing miniature horses. They would need a smaller space and less feed, and also she could transport them in the back of her covered truck which is a Nissan pickup with a cap. It was with this that she got Apple Dumplin'. A lady in New York had two minis for sale as she no longer wanted them. So Laurie and a friend arranged to buy them. They drove to Albany and brought them back in Laurie's truck. Apple Dumplin's sister now lives in New Hampshire with Laurie's friend, Annemarie.

Apple Dumplin' will never have to pull a cart or be ridden as Laurie does not believe that the horses she rescues should ever have to work. As with all the other ladies, Apple Dumplin' will live out her life being loved and cared for in the company of other little horses.

Apple Dumplin' and Foal

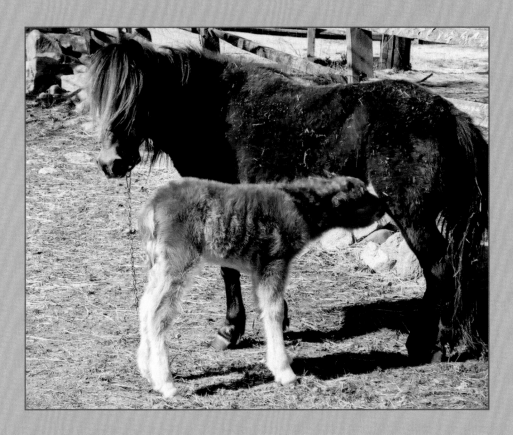

Blue

Blue is a lovely, little, white horse who was a registered mare. When she developed an eye problem, her owner paid for a very expensive portable medical scan to find the cause. The veterinarians could not find the cause or know whether this blindness would be passed on to her offspring – and there seemed no cure or correction available. As nothing could be done for Blue, her owner could not chance using her for breeding purposes and so put her up for sale.

Laurie's heart could not resist getting Blue, so she saved money to buy her, and then had to find a shipper who would pick her up in Michigan. As it turned out, the shipper who picked up Blue was the man who went to the very southern tip of Texas to pick up Missy as well.

Daily when Laurie drives out to feed the horses she toots her horn to let Blue know she is coming so she can come near the gate . The other horses seem to know Blue is blind, and while they are not exactly mean to her, they do try to eat her feed so Laurie has to be sure she gets Blue's bucket and keeps the others away from it while Blue eats the grain. Blue does seem to be able to find the hay by herself and manages to get to the water bucket. She socializes more with some of the horses than with the rest. You can sometimes see them standing close and nuzzling each other's head or neck. One of the newer horses, we will learn about later, is especially nice to Blue, and Laurie hopes this friendship will continue.

Blue

Missy

Missy, at twenty-four, is the second oldest of the group and is not a mini, but a pony. Laurie often visits web sites on minis and saw that a lady in Texas could no longer keep this spotted pony. Laurie gets in touch with the sellers by phone and mail and usually gets a picture that often tells her the physical condition the animal is in and the way they are living. She was appalled at Missy's living conditions and her shape.

Nine months after Laurie agreed to buy Missy, she finally found a willing shipper who could go to Texas. They did not know whether Missy would be able to stand the long trip to Michigan, through Canada and New York, before the delivery to Massachusetts. The shipping costs are often four or five times the price of the horse.

Now, several years later, Missy is getting back to more normal weight and shape and enjoys living and playing with her new friends. Like Blue, she settled in despite her handicap.

Missy

Frosty

Frosty, " the snow girl," is a very special young lady as she is extremely friendly. Her face is white as is most of her body though her legs have become more gray as she grows older. Laurie saw her in the want-ad section of a weekly publication – one of many related to miniature horses. She arrived in Falmouth July of 2001, and Laurie picked her up with her truck. She had been rescued from a Petting Zoo that had been closed down and that probably explains why she is so friendly with people and loves the attention they give her.

Frosty

Tara and Fawn

Fawn and Tara came in September of 2001. The advertisement for them was on the internet and they had to be shipped from New Mexico. As they had been born on a pinto breeding farm and were solid in color, not two-colored, they were culled for sale. Laurie renamed them as she did not like their names, Smoke and Fire, and she calls the one that is the reddish color of a baby deer, Fawn. She has a white blaze down her nose and two white hind feet. The other is as black as tar, and Laurie renamed her Tara.

Both had already been bred and were expecting foals, which is what baby horses are called. Laurie sold the colts off-island on the internet when she decided they could leave their mothers. She tries to be very certain the new owners will take proper care of them and love their horses as much as she does her own.

Tara

Fawn

Lady

Lady came from Florida. As it happened, she also came in September 2001. Laurie thinks she has the face of an angel. She is a chestnut pinto which means she is reddish brown with patches of another color — in her case — white. She was owned by a lady who was cutting back on her stock by getting rid of those with defects in their stature as they could not be used for show animals and might also pass the fault on to their offspring. Lady's defect is called cow hocked which means her knees do not have the proper conformation. As before, Laurie took her truck across to Falmouth on the ferry to meet the shipper and brought the horses back.

She visits them daily except the few times she has been sick or has had to work overtime. Then her daughter, Marie, steps in and carries out the chores.

Lady

Black Lily and Maisy Gray

Marie and a friend have also gone to the mainland to pick up the horses from the shipper. In January 05, they went just before the blizzard to Upton, MA to pick up Maisy Gray and Black Lily. These two were advertised in a classified sales catalogue and Laurie could not resist them.

Maisy Gray is the one who has been seen nuzzling and talking with Blue. Both these minis are small. They are closely bonded and they always seem to be together. The woman who owned Black Lily and Maisy Gray was cutting back on the number of minis she had. She knew Gus Ben David and learned about Laurie from him. So this woman was delighted for the two little ladies to come here and live the rest of their days together.

Every spring Laurie decides which five minis she can take in her truck to a pasture in Chilmark after April 15th. She rents that pasture for the summer when it is allowed by law to be used for horses as it has no shelter. She must bring them back by October 15th to their winter pasture where there are plenty of shelters.

Black Lily

Perhaps I should tell you that Laurie keeps a detailed file on each of her "girls" as she calls them and stays in touch with their former owners and people who have bought horses from her. While she plans to keep all of the minis she has now, she has had several in the past that just did not fit in, seeming to prefer to be single pets. She tries to learn as much as she can about them before buying them. And she has helped other people interested in buying minis so that they are happy with their purchase. Laurie keeps her eyes and ears open for new homes and owners that might be interested in providing loving care and a home with no demands upon their daily life.

Laurie learns about the horses on the internet and also from a weekly magazine that is especially oriented to the sale of minis. Her expenses are paid "out of pocket" which means she has to be very careful and plan ahead to have money to buy hay and grain and gas for her truck. She keeps veterinary expenses to a minimum which is why they do not come in contact with other horses and why she is learning to trim hooves. There is no money for extras like new halters. People give her used buckets. She is willing to help anyone interested in the special little horses and anyone wishing to help Laurie can get on touch with Vineyard Miniature Horse Rescue, Inc., Post Office Box 199, Vineyard Haven, MA 02568, Martha's Vineyard, Massachusetts.

Maisy Gray

Vineyard Miniature Horse Rescue, Inc.

Post Office Box 199

Vineyard Haven, MA 02568

Martha's Vineyard, Massachusetts

Lee DeVitt, author of a children's book, *A Clam Named Sam*, lives on the Island of Martha's Vineyard and became intrigued when she heard of the love Laurie had for miniature horses. Lee lived on a farm in Wisconsin where she raised chickens and sold eggs and fryers. Then her children raised lambs and took care of their own riding horses – so Lee had experience with some of the work and the challenges Laurie faces. Knowing Laurie did not have much money to do all she would like for her "girls," Lee decided to write about them with the hope that other people would become interested enough to help. She is very impressed with how Laurie has learned to manage all she does and still is learning to do more, such as trimming hooves.